Victorian To Vamp

Women's Clothing 1900-1929

Paula Jean Darnell

Fabric Fancies, Reno, Nevada

Published by: **Fabric Fancies**
P.O. Box 50807
Reno, NV 89513

Printed in the United States of America

Publisher's Cataloging-in-Publication
(Provided by Quality Books, Inc.)

Darnell, Paula Jean
    Victorian to vamp : women's clothing 1900-1929
/ Paula Jean Darnell. — 1st ed.
    p. cm.
    Includes bibliographical references and index.
    LCCN: 99-72951
    ISBN: 1-887402-15-2

    1. Fashion--History--20th century. 2. Costume--History
--20th century. I. Title.

GT596.D37 2000   391'.009'041
                    QBI99-1430

Cover design by Linda Anderson, Design Lab, Reno, Nevada

Table of Contents

In the Gay Nineties, the decade preceding the turn of the century, Victorian women wore long sleeved, floor-length dresses complemented by hats and gloves. *Delineator*, January 1897.

Introduction

The years 1900 to 1929 covered a transitional time in American society as the population shifted from rural and agricultural to urban and industrial, and Americans grappled with the problems that accompanied change. In the political arena the Progressive Era was in full swing with legislators passing numerous laws dealing with the regulation of business, the political process, and social welfare. People optimistically looked forward to the future, confident that reform would improve the country.

Women's position in society from 1900 to 1929 was changing also, but very slowly. Both the bicycle and the automobile led to new courting styles and eventually to more freedom for women. High school and college enrollments by women increased during this time, and more young women entered the workplace although, for many, their working years were a prelude to marriage. Only a few women had careers.

In the Nineteenth Century, women had been expected to concern themselves only with domestic matters. They could not vote and had limited legal rights. Even so, women were idealized because they were thought to have a higher sense of morality than men. Victorian women's clothing reflected their place in society; although frequently beautiful, their dress was extremely constricting and confining. The woman's costume of the 1800s featured a pinching corset with whalebone or spring steel stays, tight bodice, long, heavy skirt, and gloves a size too small. When fully dressed, women completely covered their bodies and only their faces and hair showed under their hats. Victorian morality dictated that a woman should not show her "limbs," and even a glance of a woman's ankle was considered shocking.

By the turn of the century, clothing had begun to change only slightly. The Gibson Girl became a symbol of America's model woman. Idealized in the drawings of Charles Dana

Gibson, the Gibson Girl possessed a beautiful face framed by a lovely hair style and often crowned with a wide-brimmed, elaborately decorated hat. She had a very peculiar silhouette because the type of corset worn at the time forced the figure into an unnatural bent position, sometime called the "Gibson bend." This style continued for almost a decade until the new mode of a straight, upright figure, which Paul Poiret, a Parisian designer, introduced, became popular. Long skirts continued to be the norm until the mid-teen years when women raised their skirts to ankle length.

By the 1920s women's clothing had changed drastically and now featured chemise-style dresses with short skirts, light-weight fabrics, and short or no sleeves. In order to look good in the waistless chemise, which had a rectangular shape, women had to have boyish figures. As they had in previous decades, women used foundation garments to achieve the ideal silhouette so that they could wear the fashionable styles.

During the transition from the Victorian times of the 1890s to the modern times of the 1920s, women's increased interest in participating in sports influenced clothing styles for, even in sports, women had been hampered by clothing that restricted their movements. The bicycling craze of the 1890s had caused a grassroots movement among women cyclists to alter their clothing so that they could cycle more easily. This was the first sign that women meant to adjust their clothing to their lives rather than their lives to their clothing. Sportswear changed very slowly also, but by the 1920s it permitted the movement needed to swim, golf, play tennis or other sports.

From the 1850s, some women had been concerned with dress reform for reasons of physical comfort, ease in movement, and as a political statement. Even after the woman suffrage supporters decided to abandon the drive for dress reform, a few women continued to agitate for dress reform. Ironically, not long after the Nineteenth Amendment became law, the reformers' wishes came true; women's clothing styles reflected a new-found freedom, a change from Victorian to modern.

6

By the early twenties, women wore their dresses at mid-calf length; later in the decade they shortened their skirts to knee length. *Designer*, July-August, 1920.

Illustrator Charles Dana Gibson's drawings idealized young women in the early years of the Twentieth Century. The scene above is part of a Gibson drawing that appeared in *Collier's*, June 13, 1903.

Women's Clothing 1900-1909

As the Twentieth Century began, the Gibson Girl epitomized fashion's ideal. Popularized by her creator, illustrator Charles Dana Gibson, who modeled her after his wife and her sisters, the Gibson Girl portrayed an image of feminine grace with her tiny, tightly corseted waist, neatly tailored bell-shaped skirt, high-collared, long-sleeved blouse, and masses of rolled and neatly pinned hair piled high on her head. A huge, heavily embellished hat held on by a long, decorative hatpin balanced this costume. Although a few of the Gibson Girl's blouses and skirts were plain, the old Victorian urge to decorate usually prevailed, and the Gibson Girl frequently lavished her clothing with lace, tiny tucks, and fancy embroidery.

The Ideal Silhouette

The most noticeable feature of the silhouette of the fashionable Edwardian woman consisted of a pouched-out blouse, sometimes referred to as the "pigeon breast" or "kangaroo pouch." With large, protruding bosom jutting out in front and hips pushed back, the Gibson Girl's figure fell into an S-shape, also known as the "Gibson bend." This peculiar shape was caused by a new type of corset invented by a French woman, Madame Gaches-Sarraute, whose intention had been to remove the great pressure exerted on the waist by the corsets then in style. This would have worked successfully if women had worn the new corset, which released the breasts and extended farther over the hips, as it had been meant to be worn. Instead women tightly laced the new corset form farther up over their breasts, which, in turn, forced the hips back and led to the prevalent S-shaped silhouette, causing an effect "as if the top of the lady was a foot ahead of the rest of her," according to Ewing's *History of Twentieth Century Fashion.*

A puffed-out "pigeon breast" typified the S-shaped silhouette that was fashion's ideal in the first decade of the Twentieth Century. *Delineator*, December 1907.

Clothing Styles

The standard costume for a woman consisted of either a dress or a skirt and blouse, usually called a waist or a shirtwaist. Although women wore bloomer pants for physical education classes and for some sports activities, pants did not exist as part of a woman's wardrobe during this time.

Dresses

Until 1904 garments usually consisted of a separate bodice and skirt hooked together at the center back. After 1904 one-piece dresses with bodice and skirt seamed together at the waistband also appeared. During this time bodices were constructed of two parts, a boned lining, which fit tightly and fastened separately, and the outer part of the bodice, which pouched out in front and was worn drooping over the waistband of the skirt in front, the back part of the bodice still being tightly fitted in the fashion of earlier bodices worn in Victorian times. Skirts were gored and fitted at the waist and over the hips; a few skirts still had trains, but these appeared less frequently than in Victorian times.

Dresses of fine, light-weight, transparent fabrics and laces characterized this time. Now referred to as "Edwardian whites" by vintage clothing enthusiasts because the most popular color for day dresses was white, dresses from this period that have survived the years are sometimes mistaken for wedding gowns.

Wealthy women romanticized spending serene late afternoon
tea time dressed in flowing, lavishly embellished garments
known as tea gowns. The drawing above shows the tea gown
described on the opposite page from the October 1902 issue of
the *Delineator*.

Tea Gowns

A garment that well-to-do women wore at home in the afternoon, known as the tea-gown, was constructed of lace and luxurious fabrics, such as silk chiffon or crepe. Since women only wore tea gowns at home, they were cut so that they were looser and more flowing than everyday garments. Nevertheless, the construction of the tea gowns indicates that even these at-home garments were meant to be worn with corsets. Tea gowns should not be confused with wrappers, which were everyday loose garments women wore around the house. Women might make their own wrappers of inexpensive cloth, and they did not need to wear corsets under them. Some fashion editors scolded women for getting into the sloppy habit of wearing a wrapper all day rather than "proper" dress.

A description in the October 1902 issue of *The Delineator* of a tea gown pattern included the following suggestions for appropriate fabric to use when making the dress:

> Scarlet crepon with bands of red or black satin would be very effective. Other appropriate fabrics are cashmere, French flannel, challis, and all the Japanese materials are in use for these gowns. A handsome development would be in lavender zenana, with trimming bands of Arabe lace over ivory white satin or silk. A sash of China or some other soft silk will give the finishing touch.

Tea gowns, although structurally cut looser than tailored day dresses or suits, were not plain, simple garments. Tea gowns called for luxurious fabrics and lavish laces, as indicated by the fabric and trimming suggestions in the description above. Writing in *The Cult of Chiffon* in 1902, Mrs. Eric Pritchard lauded "this garment of mystery which can be a very complete reflection of the wearer." She thought that the "ideal tea-gown" consisted of a garment "of accordion pleated chiffon, lace and hanging stole of regal furs" and declared that: "In our drawing rooms when the tea-urn sings at five o'clock, we can don these garments of poetical beauty."

Floor length coats were also constructed to accommodate the
S-shape lines of the prevailing dress styles of the day.
Delineator, December 1907.

14

Wraps

Women most frequently wore long coats or jackets over their dresses during this time although capes and fur stoles remained options as well. In the December 1907 issue of the *Delineator*, the fashion editor proclaimed that fur cloaks were the latest style for winter: "Furs of the highest quality are made up in wide, rippling cloaks, more like winged capes than coats...Many of the dressier pieces show a three-quarter sleeve of lace dyed to match, and draped in raglan and in sling-shaped lines." Women often carried large, pillow-sized fur muffs; sometimes the fur of the muffs matched a fur stole, which often had the head or tails of the animal still attached, or a cloth coat with a fur collar or cuffs. The muff might also be fashioned in velvet, satin, or another fabric. When a woman carried a muff, it replaced her purse because, in addition to providing a place to warm her hands, the muff contained a pouch where she could store the small objects she needed to carry with her.

Nightgown 9625, of nainsook, with
embroidery and lace

Corset Cover 7684, of handkerchiefs
with lace and ribbon

Chemise or Corset Cover 9854, of
cambric with eyelet-work and lace

Drawers 9495, of long-cloth with lace-
trimmed lawn ruffles

Combination Suit 9158, of flouncing,
beading and ribbon

Drawers 1582, of linon with insertion,
edging and medallions

Chemise and Skirt 9709, of lawn with
insertion, edging and ribbon

Corset Cover 9418, of linen with
embroidery and lace edging

Petticoat Skirt 1587, India linon, lace,
beading and ribbon

Over their corsets, women wore many other undergarments
including layers of petticoats. *Delineator*, December 1907.

Undergarments

A tight corset formed the foundation for the ideal Gibson bend silhouette. Under it all, in addition to a corset, women wore petticoats, usually of white cotton or linen with lace trim at the hems and camisoles under their waists, which were often of sheer fabric. Sometimes the two garments were combined into one with the chemise attached to bloomers, which also had an overskirt. Bodices of chemises and camisoles were puffed out in front so that they would fit properly over the corsets that forced women's figures into the S-curved, pigeon-breasted shape. Most undergarments displayed some type of trimming; many were trimmed very lavishly with combinations of lace, embroidery, ribbon, eyelet, ruffles, flouncing, lace beading, or medallions.

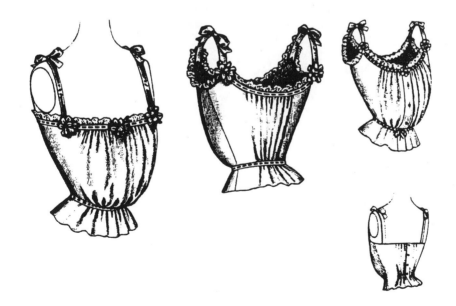

Stylish millinery was a big part of the fashion scene. Women wore hats whenever they went out. *Delineator,* December 1907.

Millinery

Women completed their outfits with gloves, hats, purses, stockings, shoes, and furs. Of all the fashion accessories, the most important to proper attire was the hat. During the early years of the twentieth century, women wore large hats. Throughout Victorian times women considered a hat or bonnet a necessary and integral part of any day costume worn outside of the home. This idea remained into and beyond the Edwardian era. Not until the 1960s did most women stop wearing hats as part of their day clothing outside of the home. The extravagant millinery of the Edwardian age drew emphasis to the women's faces and provided balance to skirts, which were narrow at the waist and flared at the hem. These brimmed, large hats extended well beyond the woman's coiffure, but women wore them so that the brim and decorations of the hat provided a kind of frame for their faces. Luxurious fabrics and lavish trims were the norm. Trimmings consisted of velvet bows and roses, braid, veiling, embroidery, ribbon, lace, and artificial flowers while feathers frequently trimmed the most fashionable hats. In the December 1907 issue of the *Delineator*, types of feather decorations recommended for modish hats included ostrich plumes, shaded cassowary plumes, aigret, and coq feathers.

Ostrich plumes, the most popular feathers used to trim hats, were rather expensive at up to five dollars per plume. A 1907 advertisement from Cawston Ostrich Farm in South Pasadena, California, offered a "selected plume...made from the finest male feathers, full and wide, long flues, strong and durable, perfect workmanship, 15 inches long, price $5.00 for black, white, or any solid color; shaded, 50 cents additional." Other companies offered the ostrich feathers at a cheaper price. One was the Chicago Feather Company, which offered by mail order a "lovely ostrich feather...beautifully curled; size 14 inches" for $1.65 plus a nickel for postage.

For women who worried about keeping up with fashion on a tight budget, changing the trimmings on a hat was a common method of keeping current. Hats could be updated more easily than dresses. With a little ingenuity, women could re-trim an old hat and transform it into a fashionable modernized accessory. A Diamond Dye advertisement from 1907 quotes a customer, Mrs. J. W. Kelly, who attained an updated look by dying the plume on her hat:

> This new hat cost me 90 cents. What do you think of my new hat? It cost me just 90 cents. I changed the shape of my last winter's hat--bought a remnant of beautiful red ribbon for 80 cents and a package of cardinal dye for 10 cents and dyed the old plume and it came out so fresh and new.

Such a solution worked well for women of modest means who wanted to update a style but could not afford to purchase a new hat.

"This new hat cost me 90c"

"What do you think of my new hat? It cost me just 90c. I changed the shape of my last Winter's hat—bought a remnant of beautiful red ribbon for 80c. and a package of cardinal dye for 10c. and dyed the old plume and it came out so fresh and new. I don't know what I would do without Diamond Dyes."

Mrs. J. W. Kelly, Boston, Mass.

Diamond Dyes Will Do It

The August 1905 issue of *Pictorial Review* featured this hat along with instructions on how to make it.

Riding in an open automobile meant that drivers and passengers needed to shield themselves from the elements. To accomplish this, women sometimes wore protective veils over their hats for motoring. *Woman's Home Companion*, July 1905.

Enter the Automobile

The early automobile started out as a "horseless carriage," but it was much faster than the horse-drawn carriage. Driving an automobile required skill rather than strength, and women liked the new vehicle because they did not have "to control a spirited, skittish team" of horses, according to James Flink's *Automobile Age*. When automobile manufacturers replaced the crank starter system with the electric starter, making the starting process much easier, women became more eager to drive.

To protect themselves from dust, heat, rain, and insects, all hazards of riding in a horseless carriage, women wore long coats or "dusters," specifically for motoring. Gloves and a hat with a long veil covering the face and tying under the chin and sometimes goggles completed the costume. A French milliner even concocted a silk and lace hood with see-through isinglass.

The fashion industry, finding a new market, was eager to cater to women drivers' needs and so were numerous other automotive businesses. According to Virginia Scharff in *Taking the Wheel*: "Clearly, women would insist on driving, just as they were demanding the right to broaden their horizons in other regards. It seemed just as clear to many of the men who made motorcars that differences between males and females would have to be taken into account, from the inside of the vehicles out, from engine to upholstery and paint." Clever marketers of automobiles and related products took women's tastes and needs into account when designing products.

Cars were open until the 1920s when the enclosed car became the standard for the automobile industry. In 1919 about ten percent of all the cars built in the United States were closed, but by 1927 the number had increased to over eighty-two percent. This meant that a special costume was no longer required by women drivers or passengers, who could now wear whatever type of clothing the weather and occasion required without having to worry about road dust and the other hazards that went along with driving in an open car.

Wearing a motoring cap with visor, Ada Mullican Darnell, accompanied by three of her children, drove this decorated open car in a parade circa 1909. *Darnell family photo.*

This Columbia automobile advertisement features a woman in driving attire. *Collier's*, July 4, 1903.

Shown here is a typical two-piece gown described on the opposite page. *Delineator*, October 1902.

Paper Patterns and Home Dressmaking

Paper sewing patterns to make clothing construction easier for the woman who wanted to sew her own clothes had been available since the 1860s when Ellen and William Demorest and Ebenezer Butterick began aggressively marketing them. Most women owned sewing machines and made their own clothes although well-to-do women were able to afford dressmakers. The Butterick Company, which is still in business today, published a fashion magazine, *Delineator*, to promote sales of its paper patterns. In the October 1902 issue of the *Delineator*, a typical waist (bodice) pattern is pictured, offered at "20 cents; 7 sizes, 30 to 42 inches, bust measure" along with a coordinating skirt offered for "25 cents; 7 sizes, 20 to 32 inches, waist measure." This outfit was described as:

> A charming gown suitable for afternoon teas, receptions, etc.,...here shown in turquoise-blue silk bearing a conventional design, white silk and mousseline, narrow black velvet ribbon, applique lace and chiffon ruffling edged with juby trimming...The bodice has an odd feature in the jaquette that shapes a point in front. It blouses over a velvet belt, and a pointed yoke striped with the velvet ribbon is introduced. A centre-back closing is arranged, and the sleeves have voluminous puffs confined by bands. A straight collar completes the neck, the application of the trimming giving the effect of the yoke and collar being in one. Tunic skirts are once more to the fore, and a smart exponent of prevailing styles is here depicted. The skirt proper is of the five-gored flare order in frou-frou effect at the lower edge and having narrow circular flounces. It has a habit back and is in sweep length only. The tunic or upper skirt is in five gores, and the lower edge is cut in point, prettily revealing the flounces.

To aid the home sewer, the *Delineator's* editor also included further suggestions for types of fabrics and trimmings in the description:

A stylish reproduction would be in silver-gray nun's veiling over a foundation of white or self-colored taffeta. The jaquette might be of Renaissance lace, and a fold of blue panne at the top of the collar would be pretty. Albatross, voile, satin Liberty, Louisine, foulard and fancy silks and silk and wool fabrics are advised, with trimmings of fancy braid, motifs of Arabe or Irish lace, juby ruches, etc.

Butterick, the publisher of the *Delineator*, was not the only company to issue paper patterns although it was the largest and one of the oldest. Other women's magazines offered fashion advice, illustrations of the latest styles in women's clothing, and also sold tissue paper patterns for these styles via mail order. A typical page in *Pictorial Review* from August 1905 shows two "charming promenade toilettes." Tissue patterns for the waist and skirt cost fifteen cents each, and it was further noted that: "These models will be cut in pinned paper patterns, if desired, in stock sizes at the following prices: waists, $1.50; skirts $1.50; entire costume, $2.50; cut to special measure, each, 50 cents extra."

The *Pictorial Review* patterns also contained suggestions for appropriate fabrics and trimmings to construct these pieces as well as the yardage required to make each outfit. The two "promenade toilettes" in *Pictorial Review* shown on the opposite page call for "7 ½ yards of 54 inch material and 1¼ yards of allover lace" and suggest silk, wool, linen, or cotton fabric and "15 yards of 32 inch material" suggesting "figured foulard and allover lace." The various pattern services made the latest fashions accessible for anyone who could sew or employ a dressmaker.

Women's magazines offered sewing patterns so that women could make the same outfits they saw pictured in the periodicals. Shown here are two examples: "charming promenade toilettes" for which the *Pictorial Review* sold patterns. August 1905.

Department stores flourished in cities during the early years of the Twentieth Century. This John Wanamaker advertisement ran in the December 1907 issue of the *Delineator*.

Department Stores

Although most women still made their own clothing or had their dresses sewn for them by dressmakers, some ready-made clothing was available during this decade. Department stores gained in importance as the numbers of the middle class grew. People in rural areas could obtain goods via mail order from such companies as Sears, which began its mail order business in 1893, but America was moving rapidly from an agricultural economy to an industrial economy, and more Americans were migrating from rural areas to the cities. There commerce flourished, and a woman could buy a ready-to-wear garment at a retail shop or department store. However, standardized sizing was unknown, and the elaborate Edwardian styles, such as blouses trimmed with lace were not as easy to manufacture as plain skirts or wraps. Sometimes women bought garments and then added the trims themselves or bought a partially finished garment and had the department store's dressmaker finish it.

Before 1910 most manufactured women's garments available as ready-to-wear consisted of wraps, such as capes and cloaks, or corsets and other undergarments. Stores operating in this era also provided custom millinery and dressmaking services at lower prices than their smaller competitors. The convenience of using a custom dressmaker in a department store appealed to women who could also select trimmings and fabrics from store stock at the same location. This system, along with the rise of less expensive and readily available manufactured women's clothing in the years after 1910, led to a drastic decrease in the numbers of individual dressmakers and milliners, many of whom worked in their own homes or visited their customers' homes for consultations and fittings.

Aside from undergarments and outerwear, women's blouses, or shirtwaists, were the first women's garments to be mass produced. Skirts, gloves, and dresses were added to manufacturers' offerings, but department stores continued to offer custom services, mainly in an effort to appeal to the wealthier customer. Department stores also offered alteration services for the new manufactured garments since they were often ill-fitting. However, a ready-to-wear dress, even after minimal alteration charges had been added to the purchase price, was still less expensive than a custom-made garment and thus appealed to the middle-class store customer.

Women also liked the atmosphere the department stores provided. Stores, such as Macy's in New York, Filene's in Boston, and the White House in San Francisco, were spacious with luxurious goods temptingly displayed, and they catered to women's desires to have the latest fashion. Both custom departments and manufacturers of women's ready-to-wear copied designer styles from Paris so that they could boast "the latest from Paris" in their advertising. Department stores' marketing strategies consistently appealed to the up-scale customer, and this self-placement at the upper end of the retail trade continues today. The strategy did not preclude middle-class women from shopping in a department store, but it made them feel they were experiencing a bit of luxury just by shopping in fine stores, which catered to the fashionable woman.

BERGDORF AND GOODMAN Co

announce the opening of their new establishment at 616 Fifth Avenue, between 49th and 50th Streets, and take this opportunity of thanking you for your patronage to which they owe so much of their success and assure you they will earnestly endeavor to merit a continuance of your favor.

B. Altman & Co.

FIFTH AVENUE - MADISON AVENUE

34th and 35th Streets   NEW YORK

B. Altman & Co. announce that the new addition to their Store, fronting on Madison Avenue, will shortly be opened to the public. In anticipation of this important event, large and comprehensive assortments of new Merchandise for the Autumn Season have been secured.

The Services of the Mail Order Department are at the disposal of patrons residing out of town. A copy of the Autumn and Winter Catalogue will be mailed upon request.

All Charged or Paid Purchases (including heavy and bulky shipments) will be forwarded Free of Charge by mail, express or freight to any point in the United States. The methods of shipment are optional with B. Altman & Co. and no discounts are allowed.

All Charged or Paid Purchases not exceeding twenty pounds in weight will be forwarded Free by mail to all Territories, Possessions or Foreign Countries where Parcel Post rates apply.

This B. Altman advertisement offers the store's merchandise by mail order for out-of-town customers. *Vogue*, October 1, 1914.

Swimming in a Victorian bathing costume was extremely difficult due to the drag produced by all the excess yardage. *Harper's Bazar*, July 26, 1884.

The Influence of Sports on Women's Clothing

Women's participation in sports eventually influenced their clothing although during the 1800s women made few adaptations in their clothing so that they could move with ease when playing a sport. Pictures in Victorian magazines show women skating, golfing, and playing tennis or croquet dressed in their everyday clothes; the only indications from their costumes that they were intended as wear for sports were decorations on the clothes; for example, tennis racquet appliques on an outfit worn to play tennis. Even Victorian riding habits and swimming suits took the form of dresses, and this trend continued into the early 1900s.

Women's participation in such genteel sports as tennis, golf, and croquet were approved by society, but since it was considered unladylike to perspire, and because their clothes prevented it, these sports as played by women in the 1800s were not vigorous exercise. Physicians worried about whether or not women actually should exercise at all, and they wrote many journal articles on the subject of women and exercise. By the mid-1890s when thousands of American women took to bicycling, most physicians supported moderate exercise for women.

Secondary schools, colleges, and universities began adding physical education to their curricula for girls. A student who engaged in "gymnastic exercises" was careful "to have every inch of her anatomy covered by a decorous but hardly decorative 'gym suit,' which consisted of bloomers and a sailor-type or middy blouse," according to the *Pictorial History of American Sports*. However, that did not mean that the schools or instructors encouraged competitive play for women; in fact, many school officials actively discouraged or prevented women from participating in competitive sports. In 1894 the faculty of Vassar turned down an invitation from the students of Bryn Mawr for a tennis match between its students and the students at Vassar, and in 1904 The Midwest Conference of Deans of Women went on record as disapproving women's intercollegiate competition in the United States. Despite resistance from the very people who would seem most likely to encourage women in athletics, women's competitive school sports did grow during the early 1900s. The philosophy of many educators was that the intense competitive spectator sports should be reserved for men with the women's role confined to that of spectator or cheerleader. Female physical education instructors encouraged informal play days for women rather than aggressive physically demanding contests.

Many people still objected to watching a woman exercise; they did not want to see a woman perspire, have her hair out of place, or show her legs. Pierre de Coubertin, the founder of the modern Olympic Games, strongly objected to allowing women to participate in the Olympics. His statement in 1912 sums up his lifelong belief that the Olympics should be for men only: "We feel that the Olympic Games must be reserved for men...we must continue to try to achieve the following definition: the solemn and periodic exaltation of male athleticism with internationalism as a base, loyalty as a mean, art for its setting, and female applause as reward." Women were barred from the first Olympics in 1896. After the 1896 Olympics, women slowly made inroads, first with unofficial archery competition, and later with official sanction. Until his death in 1937, Coubertin continued to oppose women's participation in the Olympics: "Let women participate in all sports if they wish, but let them not exhibit themselves in doing so."

The changes that women made to their dress during the 1890s so that they could ride bicycles were especially significant in establishing a trend that took another twenty-five years to develop fully, but that changed women's views of dress and the way they wore clothing. For the first time, during the heyday of the bicycling craze of the 1890s, women by the thousands insisted that they would ride bicycles, and it was a first step towards both toward greater independence in their lifestyles and eventually a freer form of clothing. Women realized that bicycling would be much easier if they could change their costumes to accommodate the needs of the sport rather than trying to adapt the sport to accommodate cumbersome clothing.

Named for Amelia Bloomer, who had worn a costume of loose Turkish-style trousers as a symbol of the women's suffrage movement in the 1850s, bloomers were adapted for use as women's bicycling costumes in the 1890s. Because of its political connection, the bloomer costume had always been controversial. Even in the 1890s, although the women of the suffrage movement had long since given up wearing bloomers as a symbol of the cause, many people had not forgotten the link, and they objected to female bicyclists wearing it for cycling. Others objected on the grounds that a bloomer outfit was neither a seemly nor a modest enough costume for a proper Victorian lady to wear.

As the century drew to a close, women cyclists were back in skirts, but these cycling skirts were much shorter than the ground-sweeping ones that women wore for cycling at the beginning of the decade. A lasting influence of the cycling costume adaptations of the 1890s was that a trend had been established for more rational dress for women. In this instance, costume changes seemed to stem from women's grass-roots reactions to the challenges of cycling rather than from following a style introduced by famous women sports participants, as happened with swimming suits and tennis wear.

Women professional baseball players wore uniforms that changed somewhat throughout the period between 1890 and 1920. An 1898 article in the *Reading Eagle* described Lizzie Arlington, a well-known female pitcher, as wearing "a gray uniform with skirt coming to the knees, black stockings and a jaunty cap." It was also reported that, "her hair was not cropped short, but was done up in the latest fashion." Another player, Alta Weiss, started her baseball career in 1907, wearing long skirts and wrote to her mother that she was forced to play in her long blue skirt, which "is about all in" because "my others are all too short." By the following season, Weiss was appearing in bloomers that came to a few inches below her knees. Lizzie Murphy, a player with the Boston All-Stars wore bloomers during the early days of her career, but by the time she signed with the All-Stars in 1918, "she wore the regular baseball uniform of the day: a peaked cap, heavy wool shirt, wide belot, baggy pants, thick stockings and stirrups, and glove," according to *Women in Baseball.* Her uniform differed from that of the men on the team because hers had her name stitched in large letters on the front and back of the shirt. She was billed as the team's star, and this left no doubt as to who Lizzie was when the fans came to see a game.

Tennis was one game that was always considered proper for a lady to play, but her costume and her equipment made it very difficult to do so. Victorian tennis costumes began as "ground-length skirts, petticoats, and steel-boned corsets," which had "collars up to their chins and sleeves down to their wrists," according to Billie Jean King. Their tennis rackets were both heavy and loosely strung, making a hard service or volley nearly impossible. Laura Outerbridge, the sister of Mary Outerbridge who is credited with introducing tennis in the United States, described preparations for the game, which was held at the Staten Island Cricket and Baseball Club: "Miss Krebs, sister of the president of the cricket club, became an interested operator and coaxed us to give up the long dresses worn at the time, which touched the ground at the back. So we provided ourselves with flannel dresses to the tops of our boots."

Helen Hotchkiss Wightman, known as the "Queen Mother of Tennis" because she taught many future women tennis champions to play, influenced the change in women's tennis from a non-strenuous activity, in which it was considered unladylike to run after the ball, to a competitive sport for women. In 1902 she was sixteen years old when she embraced the sport. To practice on the only asphalt court available in Berkeley, California, where she lived at the time, she had to appear at five o'clock in the morning because females were not permitted to play after eight o'clock." She was the first woman to introduce net play, and she frequently appeared in sleeveless dresses so that she would have more freedom of movement to serve and volley. Her skirts were not ground-sweeping but ankle length. This was about as far as one dared to go in the early Twentieth Century. Not until two decades later did women competitive tennis players substantially shorten their skirts to allow for easier movement on the court.

In the first decade of the Twentieth Century, tennis costumes followed the same lines as day dresses. *Harper's Bazar*, July 1907.

Many people associated bloomers with the woman suffrage movement and objected to them on political grounds even when they were used for bicycling. *Delineator*, August 1894.

Except for their decoration, these yachting outfits differed little from day dresses. *Pictorial Review*, August 1905.

Bloomers were named for Amelia Bloomer who popularized the dress reform movement in the 1850s by writing about it in her newspaper, the *Lily*. She also advocated other reforms, proclaiming: "Woman has a right to vote for civil officers, to hold offices, and so to rule over men."

Dress Reform

The clothing reform movement, which culminated in the shorter and lighter garb of the 1920s, had its roots in the Nineteenth Century. Victorian women's clothes, with their tight corsets, bustles, hoops, wire cage skirt supports, and long skirts, severely restricted free movement.

Clothes reflected society's views of women's roles. The ideal Victorian woman was a decorative ornament in her husband's house. Her constitution was thought to be weak and delicate. Her concerns were supposed to be her home and family. Her education need not be advanced but should be sufficient so that she could play the piano and sing a little, dance, do needlework, and participate in light, amusing conversation.

Her status, mandated by law and cemented by churchmen's interpretation of religious scriptures, was that of a citizen who had few rights. Women had no voting rights and little control over their own property.

Ironically although women were denied political and property rights and the churches held that women were creatures meant by God to be subservient to men, society also held the romantic view that women were naturally purer and of a higher moral character than men. In an 1826 issue of the *New Harmony Gazette*, a publication of that Indiana utopian community, a writer expressed the prevailing sentiment about the character of women: "She is the purest abstract of nature that can be found in all its works. She is the image of love, purity, and truth; and she lives and moves in all who possess virtuous innocence." Women were simultaneously worshiped and enslaved, and their restrictive clothing symbolized their position in Nineteenth Century society.

Amelia Bloomer popularized the first woman's dress reform costume in the United States. A staunch advocate of both the temperance movement and woman suffrage, Bloomer wore the reform costume herself and urged other women to adopt it. The Bloomer costume consisted of a short dress worn over loose pantaloons, which were gathered at the ankles. In an age of wide hoop skirts, this costume was considered outrageous and even indecent. Bloomer, a resident of Seneca Falls, New York, and publisher of the *Lily*, a journal devoted to women and reform causes, urged women to wear bloomers. Many suffrage advocates wore them, and they came to symbolize the suffrage movement. Many of the women associated with the suffrage movement were also allied with other reform causes, especially abolition before the Civil War and the temperance cause later.

Women appearing in public in the new costume, even in so presumably sophisticated a city as New York, precipitated flurries of excitement, minor stampedes of boys and young men, rude jeers, nose-thumbing, and occasionally literal mud-slinging. Tired of the ridicule and abuse, the reformers returned to wearing the same clothing as other women, but decades later when women bicyclists wore bloomers to make that sport easier and safer, people still associated the bloomer costume with woman suffrage.

Not much was heard from clothing reformers during the early twentieth century. Most women in reform movements continued to concentrate their efforts on suffrage and temperance issues; however, a few made their own independent statements of dress reform.

Dr. Mary Walker, an early and very active dress reformer, never gave up wearing reform clothing. Until her death in 1919, Dr. Walker, who won the Medal of Honor for her service during the Civil War, continued wearing her own version of rational dress, which consisted of trousers as part of an outfit that strongly resembled a man's suit.

Anna G. Noyes, a writer, complained in 1907 that although fashion changed frequently, "its incessant changes do not give an ever-increasing amount of convenience, comfort, and beauty." She wanted fashion changes to bring improved modes of dress and saw no point in buying new clothes simply because they were the latest style. She claimed that she was not looking for "something new" but "only for something good."

Noyes designed and constructed her own clothes to solve what she saw as several different problems with clothes. She reduced the weight of her costumes, shortened her skirts, and wore only two pieces of underwear instead of the usual six.

She also designed clothes with pockets. Noting that men didn't carry purses, she made her goal "to provide pockets, enough of them so that I should not have to hook on a bag or carry one." Noyes also wanted "to design a convenient method of putting my dress on and off, so that I should not have to depend upon my husband even for that." The garments she designed accomplished these goals:

> They fasten with hooks and eyes under the pleat at the left, opening from the yoke to about eight inches below the waist. In this I keep my watch, fountain pen and pencil, all securely fastened so that I shall not lose them.

A new-found freedom was Noyes' reward for her own personal dress reform. Having made her outfits much lighter, somewhat shorter, and easier in which to move, she exulted in her new-found freedom:

> In these dresses I feel like a spirit! Nothing holds me to the earth. I feel as if I had left the cocoon of the chrysalis and were learning to fly...I want to bend and twist and turn and jump and skip...just because I can! I know no buttons will burst off when I expand my lungs. No steel will snap when I stoop from the waist to touch my toes. No waist will separate from a skirt when I stand on tiptoe and stretch.

Although Noyes admitted that her ideas on dress reform were in flux, she was pleased that she was able "to go about my business in a comfortable dress." Her way of dressing provided the freedom that other dress reformers had advocated in the past.

Dr. Mary Walker insisted on continuing to wear pants as part of her own version of a reform costume long after most other early reformers had returned to wearing long skirts. *Circa 1901 photograph courtesy of the Oswego County Historical Society, Oswego, New York.*

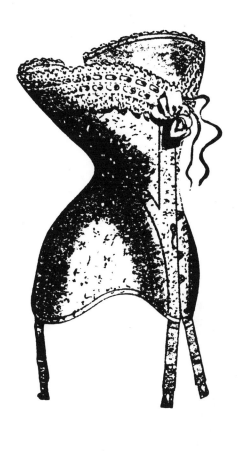

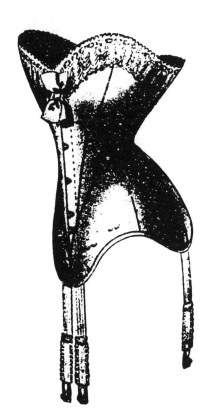

Although tight corsets, such as these shown in a Royal Worcester Corset Co. advertisement, pinched women uncomfortably, they regarded them as a necessity to wear so that they could maintain a fashionable look. Anna G. Noyes objected to corsets and advocated freedom of movement within their own clothing for women. *Woman's Home Companion*, April 1906.

Poiret's lampshade tunic made fashion headlines, but it was hardly an everyday style since most women regarded it as too avant garde even to consider wearing. *La Gazette du Bon Ton.*

Women's Clothing 1910–1919

The S-curved, pigeon-shaped silhouette gave way to a straight, upright silhouette starting around 1908, and by 1910 women had adopted the new line for their clothing. The impetus for this change initially came from Paul Poiret, a Parisian designer.

Paul Poiret

Born in 1879 in Paris, Paul Poiret began his career in fashion at nineteen when he became an assistant to the well-known designer Jacques Doucet in the late 1890s. Poiret opened his own Paris shop in 1903 and dominated the Parisian fashion scene after his meteoric rise to fame. He became well known in Europe and the Americas and, despite having to interrupt his design career to serve with the French army in World War I, Poiret was the dominant designer of the decade. In 1908 Poiret banished the "S" shape silhouette by introducing a new straight, narrow line in dresses. For the first time in decades, women's clothing did not need to feature a tiny, pinched-in waist to be fashionable. By 1912 women wore straight skirts, dresses with vertical lines, and high waistlines. This new silhouette dominated the decade of 1910-1919, during which women wore very few full-skirted dresses.

Poiret was also responsible for creating the hobble skirt, which was so narrow at the bottom that a woman wearing one could not walk naturally but had to hobble along. Dressmakers copying the Paris design solved this problem by adding pleats or slits to skirts to make movement easier.

Another Poiret invention was called a "lampshade" tunic. This consisted of a top that fell below the hips and was wired in its hem to make it stand out from the skirt, creating the effect of a lampshade. Costumes Poiret designed for the theater were influenced by his love for bright colors and the costumes of the Orient. He showed harem pants that were loose and flowing as an alternative to skirts, and although the style did not catch on with most women, his flair and imaginative use of vivid color were widely celebrated.

In 1913 a fashion editor for *Harper's Bazar* proclaimed:

> Paul Poiret is the most advanced and the most remarkable exponent of women's fashions and apparel of the present day. He is characterized by the one statement invariably made in Paris when you speak of Poiret--"*Mais Poiret--c'est un artiste--!*" Poiret is not a dressmaker. With a keen eye for colour, a remarkable ability to delineate "*la ligne,*" and above all that freedom from time-worn and conventional tendencies in fashions, Poiret is undoubtedly the greatest French authority on dress.

Fashion illustrations accompanying this article showed costumes designed by Poiret that were available in the United States from department stores, such as John Wanamaker and J. M. Gidding & Co. These dresses featured rich colors and fabric, such as a gown "from an Oriental miniature of the Queen of Sheba" which was made of "brocaded satin in the deep, rich sapphire shade combined with white chiffon" covered by a tunic "of gold lace and jewels." Descriptions of all of the gowns mentioned an Oriental influence, such as a "gown of black and canary shaded velvet with a tunic of black tulle" in which Poiret had reproduced "features in the Byzantine frieze of the Church of St. Sophia at Constantinople."

Because he pioneered both the boutique and the designer ready-to-wear system, in which the designer received a royalty for each garment sold rather than one set price for the sale of a model garment, Poiret was really the first couture designer who dared to be different, and thus his influence continues in fashion today.

The deep collar of ermine used by Doucet on his theatre frock of tapestry blue charmeuse is a luxurious touch which makes a simply-fashioned frock very dressy.

This blue serge frock seen at Longchamps was distinguished by knowing touches in the mousseline de soie undersleeves, the fancy braid buttons and ornament, and the narrow gold cord edging the girdle.

Other designers showed styles with long tunics worn over straight skirts. *Harper's Bazar,* November 1913.

A tunic dress worn over a skirt was a very popular style in the mid-teens. *Designer*, October 1917.

Clothing Styles

The dominant line of the decade consisted of a slender, narrow, tubelike design with a high waistline, and there was a trend toward more simplicity in decoration as well as in line. Of course, variation on the long silhouette abounded with much layering and skirts that basically conformed to the ideal straight line but that were somewhat looser.

Dresses

The four major dress styles were the one piece dress, which usually fastened with hooks and eyes at the center back of the garment, the skirt and blouse combination, the tunic worn over a long skirt, and the suit, which consisted of a separate jacket and skirt.

A well-known dress style from this era was the lingerie dress, made of thin white cotton. Under this, women could wear a colored slip or underdress so that they could use the same outer dress to expand their wardrobes into many different costumes. Waistlines, which fell just below the bust, were very high during the early part of the period. By 1915 waistlines had dropped to approximately two inches above the natural waistline, and by 1919 waistlines were at their natural level. The trend continued downward into the 1920s when dropped waistlines to the hip were common, and many dresses had no waistlines at all. There were only a few exceptions to these trends in waist placement with some dresses featuring dropped waistlines as early as 1915. The V-shaped neckline became common, sometimes with a fabric or lace inset that cut horizontally across the V, making a more modest neckline. Long, fitted sleeves were the norm for day dresses and suits.

For a brief time in mid-decade, designers tried to interest women in wider skirts featured in fashion and dressmaking magazines as well as department stores. Despite the designers' attempts to introduce a new trend, women did not widely adopt these styles, and the straight skirts, which by the end of World War I had risen to ankle level, continued their popularity.

These 1910 suits show the new straight, upright silhouette that dominated women's clothing in the second decade of the Twentieth Century. *Ladies' Home Journal*, September 15, 1910.

The mid-decade attempt by designers to widen skirts failed to capture women's interest. *Vogue*, May 1915.

This Doeuillet-designed black satin evening gown features a
short train. *Delineator*, September 1917.

Evening Wear

In the first decade of the century, evening wear was mainly distinguished from day wear by a lower neckline, more luxurious fabrics, and more trim. From 1910 until 1920, sleeve length became a distinguishing factor. Women wore evening clothes with no sleeves or short sleeves, above elbow length. Many skirts featured uneven hems or fishtail trains. Luxury fabrics in silk and satin continued to be popular, and the most popular trim was beading. Ostrich feathers, which had been used for millinery previously, trimmed many evening gowns during this decade.

Lenora Mullican wore a white lingerie dress in this photograph circa 1916. *Darnell family photo.*

The Lingerie Blouse

The lingerie blouse, also known as the "pneumonia blouse" became a signature piece of the period. Made of light, transparent fabric, such as fine cotton voile, these blouses featured V-shaped or rounded necklines until about 1913 when a low, square neckline, which featured rectangular-shaped lapels bordering it, became usual. Ministers, physicians, and journalists all objected to the shocking style, but that did not stop women from wearing these delicate, filmy blouses. Ministers condemned the lingerie blouse as immoral; physicians warned that it would make women more susceptible to diseases, such as pneumonia; journalists enjoyed poking fun at a fashion that aroused so much controversy.

The Frolaset Corset

A Corset That Laces In Front

Fashion stipulates that the lines of the figure should portray those of the perfectly proportioned feminine form. To attain this end, care must be exercised in the selection of a corset. The garment should be correctly designed and properly fitted. The Frolaset front lacing corset is suggested for your consideration.

Your dealer can probably show you the new Frolaset fall models.

$3.50 to $40.00

FROLASET CORSET CO.

Makers of Front Lacing Corsets Exclusively

DETROIT, MICH.

New York
Fifth Avenue Bldg.

Paris
16 Sainte Cecile

This Frolaset Corset Company advertisement ran in various issues of *Vogue* in 1914.

The New Corset

To support the new straight line in clothing, a different corset was needed, and corset manufacturers lost no time in accommodating the style. Corsets to be worn with the slender, straight dresses were very long and shaped like a tube, which began under the bustline and ended well below the hip. They had garters attached to them so that women could hold their stockings up by hooking them to a garter. A corset advertisement for W. B. Reduso Corsets in the September 15, 1910, issue of the *Ladies' Home Journal* shows this long, straight style of corset which extended to mid-thigh and claimed to accomplish the "remarkable reduction of one to five inches in the measurement of hips and abdomen, without pressure or discomfort" while at the same time giving "a full bust effect to figures of slight bust development."

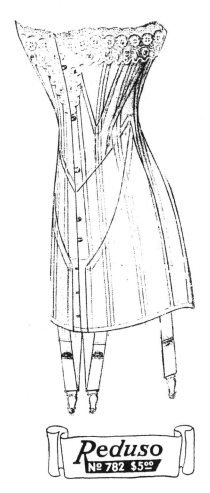

Lafarge in London made purses of beads, leather, and monkey fur. *Vogue*, September 15, 1919.

Accessories

Hats became even larger and more elaborate until around 1913 when flatter hair styles meant flatter hats as well. At their largest, hats were huge, extending beyond the wearer's shoulders and piled high with plumes and other decorations. Women secured their hats with hatpins, which came in a many decorative styles and varied in length from a couple inches to as long as a foot.

Gloves continued to be a must in every woman's wardrobe. Purses used for day were roomy so a woman could carry many articles with her, and many women made their own handbags. Evening purses from this period were beaded, framed bags, beaded reticules, or chain mesh, many of which reflected the flowing Art Nouveau style. During this time the Whiting and Davis Company obtained patents on automatic mesh-making machines. Mechanizing the process that had previously been very tedious and time-consuming handwork gave the company the ability to increase greatly production of mesh used for purses. Whiting and Davis advertised their mesh purses widely, and the company became known not only for their extensive production of purses but also for the many different variations of mesh that came to be used for purses in the next three decades.

A New Sort of Beaded Opera-Bag in Blue and Gold With a Tassel of Beads and Handles of Cords

Capelike Scarf for the Evening—Tacked at the Back and Caught by Silver Tassels—in a Changeable Chiffon of the Soft New Yellow Shot With Pink Threads and Having a Border of Yellow

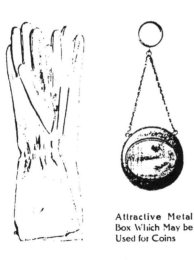

Attractive Metal Box Which May be Used for Coins

As a Vanity Box to Hold Powder This Would be Useful

Above are Chamois Gloves; on the Right is a Straw Bag Trimmed With Leather

Vanity bags and beaded purses were among popular accessories women used for special occasions. *Ladies' Home Journal*, September 15, 1910.

A 1915 Gimbel Brothers' advertisement featured hats copied from various designers. *Vogue*, 1915.

During World War I, some women's clothing displayed an armed forces' influence such as the "English military pockets" featured on this suit from 1918. *Vogue*, February 1918.

The Effect of World War I on Women's Fashions

War meant that there was a scarcity of cotton and wool fabrics, and more silk was used for women's garments. Because colored dyes were scarce, pale colors were the norm during this time. Influenced by the military, some of the dresses from this period featured sailor collars or military-style buttons.

Although dresses at the beginning of the war years tended towards frills and lace, the war period led to women adopting a slightly more practical style. A headline in the *Designer* from October 1917 proclaimed: "To the American Women Who Are True Patriots Dame Fashion Offers Many Suggestions for Economy In Her Very Latest Designs." However, a look at the featured fashions of the issue does not reveal drastic changes from the pre-war years' styles except that the skirts had risen to ankle length. This savings of fabric as well as less use of lace may have been the "economy" to which the headline referred.

War also meant that more women worked, and in war plants they did not wear dresses. It was necessary to come up with a practical type of working costume, and many wore "long, full knickers--a variation on the bloomer costume--with simple blouses, sturdy shoes, and hair-containing headgear," according to Lee Hall in *Common Threads*.

Although the opportunities that war made possible in opening up fields previously reserved exclusively for men and in higher wages quickly evaporated after the war, during the war men were forced to view women in a new light. In *Women, War, and Work: The Impact of World War I on Women Workers in the United States*, Maurine Weiner Greenwald notes that "participation in the war effort heightened the consciousness of women workers, male co-workers, managers, and government officials alike." Changes in the ways women thought about themselves continued into the next decade and influenced a new freedom in both lifestyle and dress.

Nina Wilcox Putnam advocated a form of dress that would allow women to move more easily and not require them to wear corsets to achieve fashionable figures.

Nina Wilcox Putnam and Dress Reform

In its May 1912 issue the *American Magazine* reported that Nina Wilcox Putnam, a twenty-four-year-old New Yorker, had taken up the cause of clothing "revolt, not reform." Putnam invented and adopted a new style of dress that consisted of a straight full, robe-like garment "cut of a material fifty odd inches wide...double the length from my shoulder to my instep...folded once and a slit sufficiently long to permit my head to come through a cut in the center." She finished each garment by sewing side seams, a hem and adding a "bit of braid" or embroidery. Putnam claimed that this type of dress was both comfortable, since it didn't require a corset to make it fit properly, and beautiful, since she used brocade or raw silk fabric. The dress was also easier to don because she slipped it over her head, and there was "not a button nor hook and eye" on the dress.

According to Putnam, her "honest experiment" led to disapproval from both friends and strangers:

> I am told that wearing it is an affectation, that it is a pose, a desire for notoriety. Even my best friends seem to suspect me of this. I am stared at and jeered at if I appear upon the street; and even at the opera, where I am assuredly one of the most fully covered females present, the air is so full of hostile criticism as to make me self-conscious and uncomfortable...At best, my friends excuse me on the grounds that a writer is always peculiar..."

Putnam further lamented the fact that artist friends only admired her dress "purely because of its beauty--never as a reform measure."

Writing in the *Forum* the following year, Putnam continued her clothing reform crusade, this time without reference to her own dress. Her appeal, based on economic concerns as well as concerns for physical comfort in clothes, claimed that the clothing reform movement was gaining momentum among women.

Putnam said that nobody really wanted to wear uncomfortable clothing, but that people did it simply to conform:

> That people should wear any clothing which is not exactly suited to their need and honest desires seems too ridiculous to be true, and yet that is exactly what most people do, usually without thinking of the matter. How many men really like to wear a stiff collar, or a dress suit? Or how many like to wear dark, thick suits in summer instead of a kind of glorified pajama? And women! How long will they continue to wear corsets? Not one really wants to.

She acknowledged the seductive appeal of dressing in the latest fashion: "detesting fashion, as I think the majority of us do in our most secret hearts, we are often hypnotized by it to such an extent that free action is prevented." On the other hand, she argued that clothes were simply too expensive:

> Year after year, we are made to put the money we begrudge, that we can ill afford, money we would honestly rather put into other things; money, often, that we have not got, into that particular twist to skirt or coat or hat which will keep us as ridiculous-looking as our neighbor, while, at the same time, safe from his ridicule; in other words, to save ourselves the discomforts of being out of style.

Putnam's other economic argument concerned the clothing manufacturing business. It was her idea that the long hours and poor working conditions in the industry could be redressed by clothing reform rather than by law:

> When we women first entered factories and workshops in numbers, we met unfair conditions on every side. This was particularly true of the garment trades, which were among the first to employ a great many women. And when we met this unfair treatment, women dreamed of legislating virtue into manufacturers. But it can't be

70

done! And now it is dawning upon the consciousness of a number of women that the way to reform clothing manufacturers, etc., the way to cut down insane speeding, overwork, underpay, is to change our insane conception of clothing--to strive to make it a normal, useful thing, instead of a hampering, exotic, extravagant thing, which works one group of women to death at a miserable wage because a far smaller group of parasitic women wish to be arrayed like peacocks!

Putnam protested the tactics of businessmen who continually sought to influence trends in women's fashions so that dresses would require many more yards of fabric and trim in order for textile mills to increase their profitability.

For the most part Putnam's many arguments fell on deaf ears, and she was regarded as an eccentric. However, by 1922 she found herself vindicated as clothing styles for women changed drastically.

By the early 1920s, hemlines on dresses had started to move higher. *Woman's Home Companion*, April 1922.

Flapper Style: Women's Clothing in the 1920s

By the early 1920s, a "new woman" had emerged in American society. She now had the right to vote and wanted other freedoms as well. Writing in the *Perils of Prosperity*, William E. Leuchtenburg describes her:

> The new woman wanted the same freedom of movement that men had and the same economic and political rights. By the end of the 1920s she had come a long way, though with an even longer way still to go. Before the war, a lady did not set foot in a saloon; after the war, she entered a speakeasy as thoughtlessly as she would go into a depot. In 1904, a woman was arrested for smoking on Fifth Avenue; in 1929, railroads dropped their regulation against women lighting up in dining cars. In the business and political worlds, women competed with men, though hardly on equal terms. In marriage, they edged toward a more contractual role, albeit at a glacial pace. Once kept ignorant of financial matters, they moved rapidly toward the point where they would be the chief property-holders of the country. Sexual independence was merely the most sensational aspect of the altering status of women.

The new woman's clothing also symbolized a new-found freedom. Fabrics of dresses were light, and the dresses themselves were easier to put on than the complicated styles of the past. The new woman's clothing also revealed more of her body than ever before.

For the first time fashion influence was coming from young people's clothing. Middle-aged and even elderly woman were wearing the styles made popular by rebellious youth.

Sleeveless styles became common in day wear for the first time during the Roaring '20s. *Pictorial Review*, August 1924.

These styles featured in the May 1929 issue of *Pictorial Review* were intended for the "chic matron."

This 1925 wedding photograph of Neva Darnell and James Earl Mason shows the shorter style then in vogue. *Photograph courtesy of Neva Mason and Helen and James Earl Mason, Jr.*

Dresses

The dominant style in dresses of the 1920s was short and straight with the waistline, when it existed, actually falling at the hips. Dresses were constructed so that they could be pulled on over the head or, in some cases, fastened on the side. The zipper did not come into general use until the 1930s so that any fasteners used in the 1920s consisted of snaps, hooks and eyes, or buttons. Sleeveless styles became acceptable for the first time in day wear. By mid-decade the hemline rose to the shortest level in American history up to that time, and most dresses fell slightly below the knee, but some were knee-length or even above the knee.

Variations on the straight chemise were numerous and included sashes, which women could tie in a bow at the side or in the front, making a low waistline around the hipline. Skirts were sometimes pleated from the low waistline. Dresses with lapels or ties at the neckline, godets in the skirt, or little capelets were just a few of the variations on a chemise theme.

Women favored light-weight fabrics during this time such as light woolens and silks. Many day dresses had no trimmings, but evening wear was frequently decorated with elaborate, heavy beadwork, fringe, lace, embroidery, or rhinestones. Much of the time the beadwork was sewn on a delicate silk chiffon or crepe de chine, which meant that the dress itself was very light, but the beadwork could easily add several pounds to the weight of the dress. Beaded dresses from this period that have survived until today are extremely delicate due to this combination.

The straight shape of the dresses from the 1920s meant that the ideal silhouette did not follow a woman's own natural body shape. A woman who had a flat, boyish figure fit the most fashionable mode of the day. Ironically, the shorter, sleeveless styles signaled a freedom from the repression of the Victorian Era, when even a glimpse of a woman's ankle was considered shocking, but at the same time, the straight lines of the ideal silhouette denied the true form of a woman.

Three tiers of flounces and a typical low waistline are featured
on this evening dress. *Pictorial Review*, October 1927.

Suggestions for evening gown fabrics from *Pictorial Review* included velvet, satin, and multi-colored metal brocades. October 1927.

Marie Lindsey wears a coat with typical fur collar and cuffs in this photograph circa 1923. *Lindsey family photo.*

Wraps

From 1920 to 1922 coats fell to ankle length and usually had set-in sleeves with deep cuffs and convertible collars, frequently trimmed with fur. As dresses became shorter, so did coats, and by 1925 knee-length coats were in style. Fur coats, often in the surplice style, were very popular, and college students especially favored mid-calf racoon coats with shawl collars.

For evening wear capes and coats "with dolman, batwing, and kimono sleeves were reminiscent of the exotic designs of Paul Poiret," according to Ellie Laubner's *Fashions of the Roaring '20s*. Luxuriously fabricated of velvet, silk, lame, brocade, they "were decorated with embroidery, metallic braids, tassels, or bands of fur." Other options for evening were fringed, embroidered silk shawls, Egyptian linen stoles decorated with metallic Art Deco designs, fur pieces, and ostrich feather boas.

Step-ins, also known as combinations, were convenient one-piece undergarments. *Pictorial Review*, August 1924.

Undergarments

As in the previous two decades, the undergarments women wore made attaining the ideal silhouette of the current era easier. In the twenties, because the curves of women's breasts were undesirable in achieving the ideal silhouette, women wore a foundation garment to bind their breasts so that they would appear flatter. Eventually this garment evolved into the brassiere, but its purpose in the 1920s was to flatten, not enhance, the bustline. In the April 1922 issue of *Woman's Home Companion* a typical advertisement from the Treo Company in 1922 displayed a patented elastic brassiere invented "expressly for bust-reducing." In the same magazine the H. & W. Company of Newark, New Jersey, advertised that their brassieres were "expertly designed to anticipate each prevailing mode and perfectly conform every type of figure to that mode" and that "the front panel produces a straight front line flattening in effect."

Other undergarments consisted of girdles to slim the hips, camisoles, tap pants, slips styled with the same straight lines as dresses, and "step-ins" or teddies, which combined the camisole with tap pant into a one-piece garment. Except for girdles, which used elastic or sometimes boning, undergarments were usually constructed of fine, light-weight fabric, such as cotton batiste or silk. They were trimmed with lace, embroidery, and sometimes ribbon.

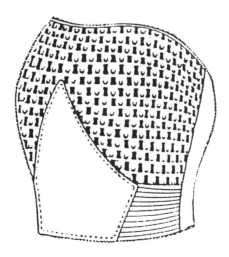

Paris milliner Agnès made many variations on the cloche.
Harper's Bazar, October 1929.

Accessories

Women bobbed their hair, cropping it very short. The cloche hat fitted over their short hair and at times hid it entirely. Sometimes the cloche had a narrow brim at the bottom, but frequently it was brimless. Although women wore turbans and picture hats in the early years of the decade, the cloche style dominated millinery during the 1920s. For evening wear, fashionable women sometimes wore little beaded skullcaps or simply a band around their heads that came across the forehead.

Women carried small, delicate purses for evening. Shaggy bead reticules, intricate glass- or steel-beaded framed purses, and mesh purses were the most popular styles for evening. Whiting and Davis, the manufacturing company that had perfected machinery which could produce metal mesh, made thousands of the mesh bags during this time. They used white metal, sterling, silver-plate, or, much more rarely, gold. The mesh varied from baby fine, called Dresden mesh, which was painted with pastel colored designs to armor mesh, which was flat and could be gold- or silver-toned or enameled, usually with Art Deco designs.

Instead of a purse for evening, sometimes women carried a vanity bag, a compact with a finger ring attached, or a minaudiere, which combined other make-up, usually a tube of lipstick, besides the compact, and had a tiny space for change, a small comb, or a handkerchief. Vanity bags were small purses but also had a decorative compact attached on the outside. Make-up, forbidden during Victorian times when women resorted to pinching their cheeks for color instead of using rouge, had become acceptable, and women carried it with them wherever they went. A compact became one of the few acceptable gifts that a young man could give to a young woman.

A typical accessory in jewelry consisted of a long single strand of pearls or beads, which dipped below the natural waistline. Other jewelry of the time showed an Egyptian or Art

Deco influence. King Tutankhamun's tomb had been opened
in Egypt in 1922, and designers rushed to imitate Egyptian
design motifs. Art Deco design emphasized angular, clean
lines, and manufacturers made many women's accessories,
such as jewelry, compacts, and purses, from this period in the
deco style. The geometric Art Deco design was a big departure
from the previously popular Art Nouveau style, which employed
flowing, curved lines and had influenced women's clothing and
accessories for the first twenty years of the century.

Beautiful Compacts of course...*but*
MARVELOUS POWDER, *too*

That's why the smartest women insist upon TRE—JUR

By the 1920s, make-up for women had finally become accepted. *Pictorial Review*, May 1929.

Glamorous shoes from 1929 featured high heeled pumps fabricated from luxurious materials, such as lamé, suede, lizard, and brocade. *Harper's Bazar*, October 1929.

Shoes and Stockings

By this time, the old high-buttoned and high-laced shoes had disappeared except for walking boots. Two-toned spectators and saddle shoes became popular for sportswear. For other occasions women wore pumps. T-straps, straight straps, and cut-outs were common, and heels became higher toward the end of the decade.

Rubber boots are especially associated with the Twenties. These galoshes had metal buckles in front, but young women did not buckle them, and the flapper took her name from these flapping boot buckles.

Stockings from the 1920s were fabricated of silk, rayon, or cotton. Rayon was less expensive than the finer, more luxurious and desirable silk; cotton hose were usually reserved for working around the house or for sportswear. Stockings were available in many pastel shades as well as black, white, brown, and tan colors. Many stockings had decorative weaves or embroidered designs on them.

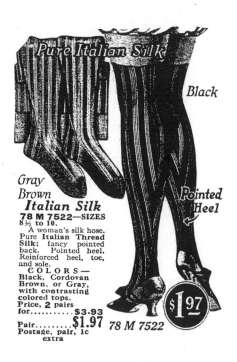

Pure Italian Silk

Black

Gray
Brown
Italian Silk
78 M 7522—SIZES
8½ to 10.
A woman's silk hose.
Pure Italian Thread
Silk; fancy pointed
back. Pointed heel.
Reinforced heel, toe,
and sole.
C O L O R S —
Black, Cordovan
Brown, or Gray,
with contrasting
colored tops.
Price, 2 pairs
for...........$3.93
Pair........$1.97
Postage, pair, 1c
extra

Pointed
Heel

$1.97

78 M 7522

Chanel wool jersey three-piece costume is on the left next to a
Lelong creation. *Vogue*, January 15, 1927.

Gabrielle Chanel

Gabrielle Chanel, the outstanding designer of the decade, adapted simplicity in classic suits and "little black dresses," both of which are still popular in fashion today. Her biographer, Axel Madsen, attributes her love for the simple styles, which have since become classic, to the fact that "she was not good at perpetual innovation." A part of the lure of Chanel's style was that "she had her workrooms execute her creations with exquisite workmanship, and in luxurious, often striking fabrics." Chanel's signature accessories--strands of faux pearls or chunky beads and quilted leather handbags with chain handles and the Chanel logo, the letter "C" entwined going both forward and backward--also remain popular today. She was the first designer to also create her own line of perfume; the most well-known of her perfumes, Chanel No. 5, is still marketed today.

Coco Chanel abhorred fads in clothing or anything that seemed eccentric. According to Elizabeth Ewing in *History of Twentieth Century Fashion*, Chanel's success was achieved "with collections featuring jersey wool dresses, straight-line classic evening gowns, often beautifully beaded, and, above all, the simple wool suits with cardigan jackets and plain or pleated skirts which have remained in fashion ever since." Chanel said, "I make fashions women can live in, breathe in, feel comfortable in and look younger in."

Although Coco Chanel died in 1971, the couture house of Chanel remains in business today. In 1990 Madsen wrote:

> Some twenty years after her death, the timeless appeal of Gabrielle Bonheur Chanel reigns supreme. The Chanel look is everywhere, canonized and copied with more fervor than ever before. Fashionable without being forward, the Chanel suit achieved new currency and appropriateness, a look that was rich, refined and, above all, dressed. Women's clothing based on gentlemanly elements, suits with jackets that fit like sweaters, masses of bogus jewelry replacing the demure real stuff, little black dresses, crisp white shirts, gold buttons, pleated

skirts, navy jackets, quilted bags, and the black-tipped sling-back shoes are staples in the wardrobes of professional women. In eclipse at those times when fashion favored eccentricity and exaggeration and in demand during periods of self-doubt and quests for certainties, Chanel's fashion is once more called eternally modern.

Chanel succeeded in adapting the straight, boyish lines of 1920s style and turning it into a costume that well-to-do professional women found appealing. Starting in the 1920s, American buyers from department stores and manufacturers bought her models and copied them. Chanel also influenced Americans with her costume designs for Hollywood films where her work promoted the boyish styles in movies during the 1920s. Women who were eager to maintain a fashionable image observed what the film stars wore and copied their clothing.

CHANEL

Chanel introduces a novel use of satin for sports wear in this black jersey cardigan costume. The green crêpe marocain blouse and facings on the jacket are striped with black satin: imported by Saks-Fifth Avenue

92

Chanel designed these coats featured in *Vogue*, April 15, 1927.

By the 1920s, bathing suits were becoming more streamlined.
Vogue, June 1925.

Sportswear

During the early 1920s women's tennis stars Suzanne Lenglen of France and Helen Wills (who was coached by Helen Wightman, the "Queen Mother of Tennis") of the United States dressed in shorter skirts. Suzanne Lenglen, a six-time champion at Wimbledon, played a graceful and calculating game of tennis. Her tennis costume consisted of a "scarlet bandeau, knee-length white pleated skirt with a sleeveless blouse," according to the *Pictorial History of American Sports*. Helen Wills, the American tennis champion, was known for her powerful strokes and great determination and concentration. She played in a "middy blouse, mid-calf-length skirt, and her trademark green-lined eyeshade," and her influence on women's tennis, which "heralded the fifty-year fight to make women's tennis a true competition sport rather than a decorative sideshow," was substantial according to March Pachter writing in *Champions of American Sport*.

Although there were changes in all women's sportswear between 1900 and 1929, the most noticeable change in costume was probably the woman's swimming suit. The bathing costume of the early Twentieth Century looked just like it had in the 1890s when it consisted of a knee-length dress with a full skirt, headgear, dark stockings, and beach slippers. Slowly this evolved until in the 1920s the suit consisted of a sleeveless, one-piece tank suit with short legs. Finally women could really swim in their swimming suits. The many yards of fabric in the skirted suits made for additional weight and great drag in the water, which meant that swimming had been difficult and and racing impossible.

Sports participation gradually became part of a more active lifestyle for women. In the Nineteenth Century, heavy clothing, sometimes weighing as much as fifteen pounds, severely hampered women's physical movement. Running, swimming, reaching, and even walking became much easier with lighter and fewer clothes that women adapted specifically for sports.

Sports clothing shown in *Pictorial Review*, August 1924.

These two photographs show the contrast in women's hiking clothes between 1900 and the 1920s. Eva Shaffer Lindsey (at top left) with relatives climbed Pike's Peak wearing a long skirt in 1900; her daughter Marie Lindsey (at left on inset) wore a short sports suit while her friend Katherine Komfala selected a sweater for hiking in the Rockies in the 1920s. *Lindsey family photos.*

Flapper style shown in *Vogue*, June 1925.

The Flapper

Who was the flapper? According to writers of the 1920s, she was a wild, young girl, who wore heavy make-up, appeared in speakeasies, smoked, drank, swore, drove fast, and professed free love. The flapper took her name from the flaps of the boots she wore stylishly unbuckled; these flapped when she walked. She symbolized rebellious youth, and her costume became part of the symbolism. Bruce Bliven, writing in an article for the *New Republic* in 1925 called her "Flapper Jane" and described her clothes:

> These were estimated the other day by some statistician to weigh two pounds. Probably a libel; I doubt they come within half a pound of such bulk. Jane isn't wearing much, this summer. If you'd like to know exactly, it is: one dress, one step-in, two stockings, two shoes. A step-in, if you are 99 and 44/100ths percent ignorant, is underwear--one piece, light, exceeding brief but roomy. Her dress, as you can't possibly help knowing if you have even one good eye, and get around at all outside the Old People's Home, is also brief. It is cut low where it might be high, and vice versa. The skirt comes just an inch below her knees, overlapping by a faint fraction her rolled and twisted stockings. The idea is that when she walks in a bit of a breeze, you shall now and then observe the knee (which is *not* rouged--that's just newspaper talk) but always in an accidental, Venus-surprised-at-the-bath sort of way. This is a bit of coyness which hardly fits in with Jane's general character.

Ironically the signature flapper dress or undress, as the disapproving called it, was readily adopted by older women also, even those who condemned the flapper's behavior. According to Bliven, the "fashion is followed by hordes of unquestionably monogamous matrons, including many who join heartily in the general ululations as to what young people are coming to."

Bliven concluded that:

...women today are shaking off the shred and patches of their age-old servitude...Woman have highly resolved that they are just as good as men, and intend to be treated so. They don't mean to have any more unwanted children. They don't intend to be debarred from any profession or occupation which they choose to enter.

Bliven was writing just twenty-five years after the turn of the century. Women who were born then, whose mothers wore skirts that touched the ground and who were not permitted to vote, had become the flamboyant flappers of the Twenties.

Very elegant flapper costumes from *Vogue*, January 15, 1927.

Abba Goold Woolson's dress reform ideas during the 1870s were far different from Nina Wilcox Putnam's clothing reform agenda in the Twentieth Century.

Nina Wilcox Putnam and Dress Reform in the 1920s

By 1922 Putnam, writing in the *Saturday Evening Post*, had concluded that "there was something wrong with my method of reform." Looking back on her days as a dress reformer, Putnam said:

> Now I was a mighty serious-minded young radical in those days, and made the mistake, common to such, of believing I could force the world to face about on any subject where I had the right of the matter...No one was with me--not even the intellectual females of my acquaintance who in those days numbered among them even such bold bad women as equal suffrage advocates. When it came to reform they all drew the line somewhere, and dress was the line. When it came to free speech, that was O.K. But free waistlines were unthinkable.

Even though her original reform costume was floor-length rather than short, Putnam admired the flapper costume and regarded herself as the first flapper because she "invented the first chemise-model gown worn in America." She also admired the flapper attitude, "the flip flapper who has too much pep to stay in when it rains." Despite outcries from conservative clergymen and writers, the chemise-style short dresses worn by flappers were accepted by society, and even "that unreasonable but extremely powerful dowager" took to the new styles, appearing in public "uncorseted, in low heels...adorned by hats that stay without hatpins and dresses that drape hookless."

Pictorial Review sold a pattern for this dress described as, "becoming to the mature figure." May 1929.

Flapper-Style Reform

For nearly eighty years dress reform ideas were ridiculed and condemned, never becoming widely accepted by society. However, women's place in society was slowly changing throughout these years. As lifestyles of women became freer, "so did...dress, and almost simultaneously with the passage of the Nineteenth Amendment that assured women of the right to vote came genuine, grass-roots changes in style," according to Doris Weatherford's *American Women's History*.

Suddenly during the 1920s a new freedom in women's clothing was born. The flamboyant flapper with her short skirts and simply styled chemise dresses symbolized a change in the role of women in society. No longer bound in tight, boned corsets or long skirts, which inhibited movement, a woman could work or play with ease.

The repressed Victorian morality of the Nineteenth Century was disappearing. The flapper was viewed as somewhat wild, not only because of her costume, but also because she smoked, drank, swore, drove fast, professed free love, and used make-up. Although the pleasure-driven young flapper symbolized women's new freedom, she was not alone. Older women wore the new clothing also: "...these flappers were not necessarily the daughters of the serene and matronly maidens in the stays of 1910. They were often the same women," according to *Mirror, Mirror: A Social History of Fashion*. Although they did not regard themselves as flappers, women who wanted to participate actively in sports, education, work, or politics enjoyed the benefits of the looser, lighter, and shorter flapper style.

The stock market crash of 1929 marked the end of the Roaring Twenties and the beginning of the plunge into the Great Depression of the 1930s when women's hemlines dropped and fashions became more body conscious. Although the flapper disappeared from the social scene, the new freedom in women's clothing continued throughout the Twentieth Century.

Bibliography

Archer, Jules. *The Unpopular Ones.* New York: Crowell-Collier Press, 1968.

Batterberry, Michael and Ariane R. *Mirror, Mirror: A Social History of Fashion.* New York: 1977.

Berlage, Gai Ingham. *Women in Baseball: The Forgotten History.* Westport, CT: Praeger Publishers, 1994.

"Bicycle Suits." *Godey's Magazine* March 1897: 442.

"Bicycling and Bicycling Outfits." *The Delineator* April 1894: 418-423.

Bliven, Bruce. "Flapper Jane." *The New Republic* 9 Sept. 1925: 65-67.

Brown, Dee. *The Gentle Tamers: Women of the Old Wild West.* Lincoln: University of Nebraska Press, 1958.

Delineator Oct. 1902.

_____ Dec. 1907.

Designer Oct. 1917.

Durant, John and Otto Bettmann. *Pictorial History of American Sports From Colonial Times to the Present.* Rev. ed. New York: A.S. Barnes and Company, 1965.

Ewing, Elizabeth. *History of Twentieth Century Fashion.* Lanham, MD: Barnes and Noble Books, 1992.

"Exclusive Poiret Costumes." *Harper's Bazar* Nov. 1913: 34-37.

Fatout, Paul. "Amelia Bloomer and Bloomerism." *New York Historical Society Quarterly* 36.4 (October 1952): 361-372.

Flink, James J. *The Automobile Age.* Cambridge, MA: The MIT Press, 1988.

Gamber, Wendy. *The Female Economy: The Millinery and Dressmaking Trades, 1860-1930.* Urbana: University of Illinois Press, 1997.

Greenwald, Maurine Weiner. *Women, War, and Work: The Impact of World War I on Women Workers in the United States.* Westport, CT: Greenwood Press, 1980..

Gregorich, Barbara. *Women at Play: The Story of Women in Baseball.* New York: Harcourt Brace & Company, 1993.

Hall, Lee. *Common Threads: A Parade of American Clothing.* Boston: Little, Brown and Company, 1992.

Hanft, Ethel W. And Paula J. Manley. *Outstanding Iowa Women: Past and Present.* Muscatine, IA: River Bend Publishing, 1980.

"Interesting People," *The American Magazine.* May 1913: 35-36.

Kerr, Rose Netzorg. *100 Years of Costumes in America.* Worcester, MA: The Davis Press, Inc., 1951.

King, Billie Jean with Cynthia Starr. *We Have Come a Long Way: The Story of Women's Tennis.* New York: McGraw-Hill Book Company, 1988.

Laubner, Ellie. *Fashions of the Roaring '20s.* Atglen, PA: Schiffer Publishing Ltd., 1996.

Leuchtenburg, William E. *The Perils of Prosperity, 1914-1932.* Chicago: The University of Chicago Press, 1993.

Macdonald, Anne L. *Feminine Ingenuity: Women and Invention in America* New York: Ballantine Books, 1992.

Madsen, Axel. *Chanel: A Woman of Her Own.* New York: Henry Holt and Company, 1990.

Merchant to the Millions: A Brief History of the Origins and Development of Sears, Roebuck and Co. Chicago: Sears, Roebuck, and Co. Publications Section, 1961.

Merington, Margaret. "Woman and the Bicycle." *Scribner's* June 1895: 702-704.

Moment, Gairdner B. and Otto F. Kraushaar, eds. *Utopias: The American Experience.* Metuchen, NJ: The Scarecrow Press, Inc., 1980.

The National American Woman Suffrage Association. *Victory: How Women Won It.* New York: The H.W. Wilson Company, 1940.

Noyes, Anna G. "A Practical Protest Against Fashion." *The Independent* 29 Aug. 1907: 503-509.

Pachter, Marc. *Champions of American Sport.* New York: Harry N. Abrams, Inc., 1981.

Pictorial Review. Aug. 1905.

Putnam, Nina Wilcox. "Fashion and Feminism." *The Forum* Oct. 1914: 580-584.

Putnam, Nina Wilcox. "Ventures and Adventures in Dress Reform." *Saturday Evening Post.* 7 Oct. 1922: 15, 93-94.

Scharff, Virginia. *Taking the Wheel: Women and the Coming of the Motor Age.* Albuquerque, NM: University of New Mexico Press, 1992.

Schwartz, Lynell K. *Vintage Purses At Their Best.* Atglen, PA: Schiffer Publishing Ltd., 1995.

Scott, Anne F. And Andrew M. Scott. *One Half the People: The Fight for Woman Suffrage.* Philadelphia: J.B. Lippincott Company, 1975.

Smith, Gene and Jayne Smith, eds. *The National Police Gazette.* New York: Simon & Schuster, 1972.

Smith, Pamela. *Vintage Fashion & Fabrics.* Brooklyn: Alliance Publishers, 1995.

Smith, Robert A. *A Social History of the Bicycle: Its Early Life and Times in America.* New York: American Heritage Press, 1972.

Sparhawk, Ruth M., Mary E. Leslie, Phyllis Y. Turbow, and Zina R. Rose. *American Women in Sport, 1887-1987: A 100-Year Chronology.* Metuchen, N.J.: The Scarecrow Press: 1989.

Snyder-Haug, Diane. *Antique & Vintage Clothing: A Guide to Dating & Valuation of Women's Clothing 1850-1940.* Paducah, KY: Collector Books, 1997.

Weatherford, Doris. *American Women's History.* New York: Prentice Hall General Reference, 1994.

White, Palmer. *Poiret.* New York: Clarkson N. Potter Inc., 1973.

Woolson, Abba Goold, ed. *Dress Reform: A Series of Lectures Delivered in Boston, On Dress As It Affects the Health of Women.* Boston: Roberts Brothers, 1874.

Woolum, Janet. *Outstanding Women Athletes: Who They Are and How They Influenced Sports in America.* Phoenix: Oryx Press, 1992.

Sources of Illustrations

Illustrations are from various issues of the following periodicals:

Chicago Mail Order Company Catalogue
Collier's
Delineator
Designer
Harper's Bazar
La Gazette du Bon Ton
Ladies' Home Journal
Pictorial Review
Vogue
Woman's Home Companion

Photographs are from the following sources:

Darnell, Doris Lindsey, Lindsey family photograph collection.
Darnell, James Roderick, Darnell family photograph collection.
Mason, Neva and Helen and James Earl Mason, Jr.
Oswego County Historical Society, Oswego, New York.

Cover art is from the following sources:

Chicago Mail Order Company Catalogue, Spring & Summer,
        1924.
Delineator, September 1899.
Designer, October 1917.
Pictorial Review, May 1929.
Stumm, Maud. Print. The Gray Lithograph Co., New York,
        1908.

Index

Books Available from Fabric Fancies

The following books may be ordered directly from Fabric Fancies, P.O. Box 50807, Reno, NV 89513. Phone orders: 775.746.0666. . Website: www.tias.com/stores/fabricfancies. E-mail: Fabricfanc@aol.com. For shipping in U.S., add $4 for first book ordered and $2 each for additional books ordered. An order form is available at the back of the book.

Victorian to Vamp: Women's Clothing 1900-1929 by Paula Jean Darnell. Covers the clothing styles of three decades, the ideal silhouettes, influences on women's fashions of sports participation, clothing designers, and what dress reformers thought about women's clothing. Illustrated with period drawings and including some photographs. Published by Fabric Fancies. Format: Softcover, 8 ½ x 11 inches, 112 pages, perfect binding.
Order number ISBN: 1-887402-15-2. $19.95.

Victorian Millinery: Ladies' Hats 1850-1900 by Paula Jean Darnell. Covers women's millinery from the 1850s through the 1890s with period illustrations and descriptions of styles of the time. Also includes some millinery patterns original to the 1800s. Published by Fabric Fancies. Format: Softcover, 8 ½ x 11 inches, 105 pages, plastic comb binding.
Order numberISBN: 1-887402-08-X. $19.95.

Victorian Bathing Costumes by Paula Jean Darnell. Bathing costumes from the 1860s through the 1890s are featured with period illustrations and descriptions of bathing suit styles. Published by Fabric Fancies. Format: Softcover, 8 ½ x 11 inches, 67 pages, plastic comb binding.
Order number ISBN: 1-887402-06-3. $19.95.

Victorian Fashions & Costumes from Harper's Bazar: 1867-1898, edited by Stella Blum. Shows costumes that were featured in period *Harper's Bazar* magazine. Published by Dover Publications. Format: Softcover, 9 3/8 x 12 1/4 inches, 293 pages, perfect binding.
Order number ISBN: 0-486-22990-4. $15.95.

80 Godey's Full-Color Fashion Plates 1838-1880, edited by JoAnne Olian. Costumes from *Godey's* magazine shown in full color. Published by Dover Publications. Format: Softcover, 9 1/4 x 12 1/4 inches, 96 pages, perfect binding.
Order number ISBN: 0-486-40222-3. $18.95

A Dictionary of Costume and Fashion: Historic and Modern by Mary Brooks Picken. A reference for over 10,000 costume and fashion-related terms. Published by Dover Publications. Format: Softcover, 6 1/8 x 9 1/4 inches, 448 pages, perfect binding.
Order number ISBN: 0-486-40294-0. $14.95.

Nineteenth-Century Costume and Fashion by Herbert Norris and Oswald Curtis. A glimpse into 1800s costume with commentary on the social milieu and activities of the period. Published by Dover Publications. Format: Softcover, 6 1/8 x 9 1/4 inches, 288 pages, perfect binding.
Order number ISBN: 0-486-40292-4. $12.95.

Authentic Victorian Dressmaking Techniques, edited by Kristina Harris. Butterick manual of vintage sewing techniques from 1905. Published by Dover Publications. Format: Softcover, 6 ½ x 9 1/4 inches, 144 pages, perfect binding.
Order number ISBN: 0-486-40485-4. $10.95.

The History of Underclothes by C. Willett and Phillis Cunnington. Describes the role played by underwear over 600 years. Published by Dover Publications. Format: Softcover, 5 5/8 x 8 1/4 inches, 272 pages, perfect binding.
Order number ISBN: 0-486-27124-2. $9.95.

Fabric Fancies Order Form

☎ **Telephone orders:** Call 1.775.746.0666. Have your credit card ready.

✉ **Mail orders:** Fabric Fancies, P.O. Box 50807, Reno, NV 89513.

▣ **E-mail orders:** www.tias.com/stores/fabricfancies

For mail orders, photocopy this form and send the copy to our address above.

SHIP ORDER TO:

Name_____

Address_____

City_____ **State**_____ **Zip**_____

Telephone_____ **E-mail**_____

Book Title	**Price**
_____	_____
_____	_____
_____	_____
_____	_____
_____	_____
_____	_____
_____	_____
_____	_____
_____	_____
_____	_____
_____	_____

Sales tax: Nevada residents only, please add sales tax
as billed in your county. _____

Shipping: Please add $4 for first book and $2 for each
additional book. _____

Total: _____

Payment is by: ☐ check   ☐ money order
              ☐ VISA   ☐ Mastercard

Card Number:_____

Name as it appears on credit card:_____

Expiration date:_____